# Story Time

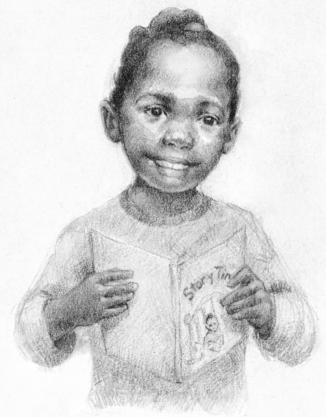

Written by Polly Peterson

Illustrated by Nneka Bennett

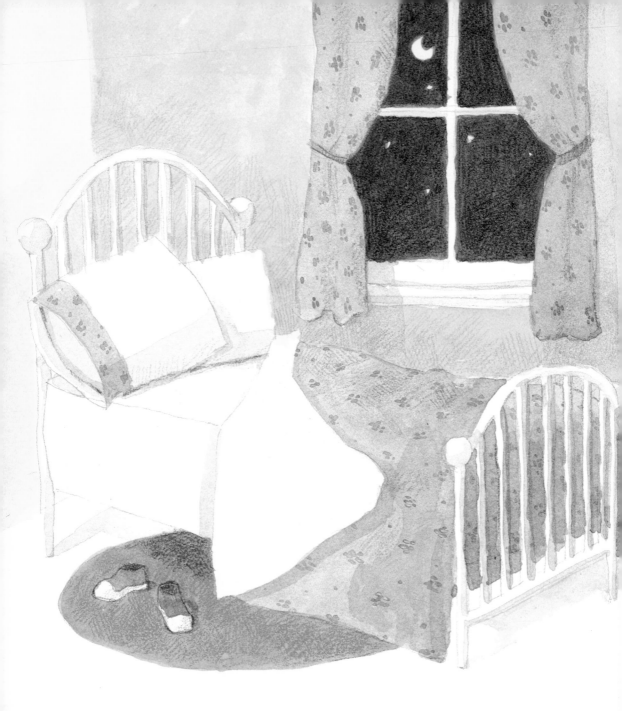

Here is my bed.

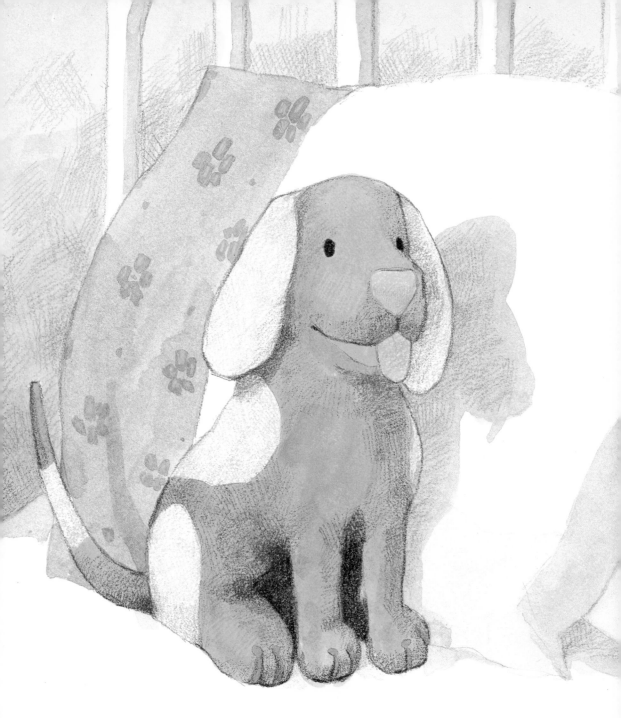

Here is my dog.

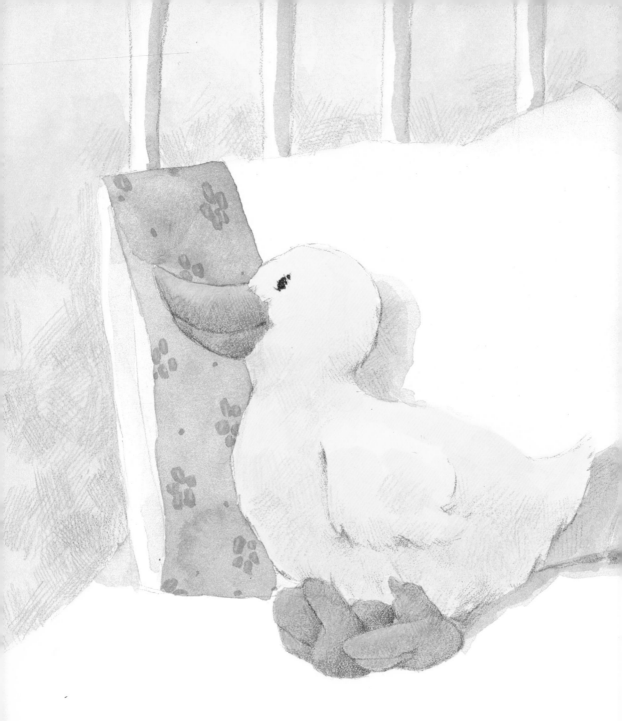

Here is my duck.

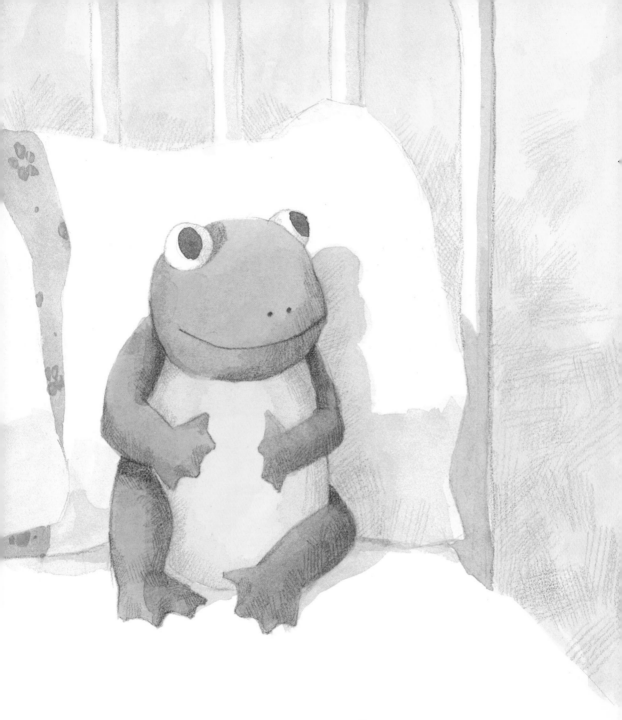

Here is my frog.

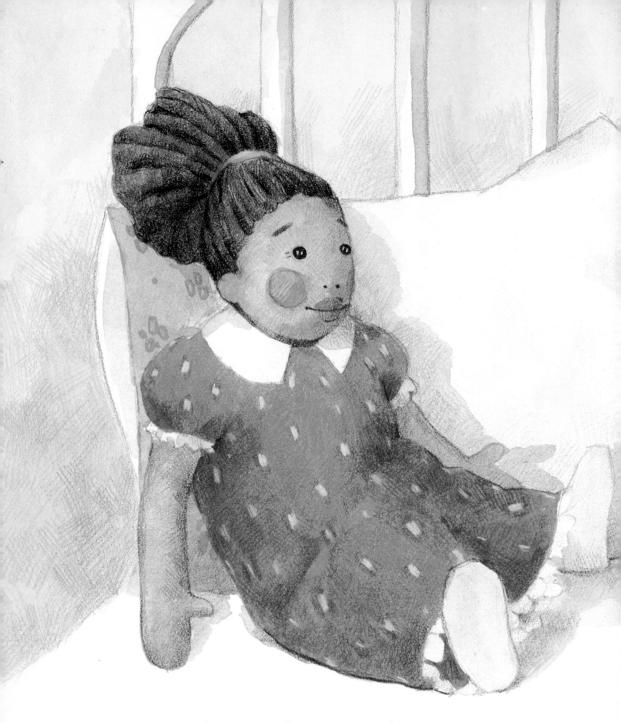

Here is my doll.

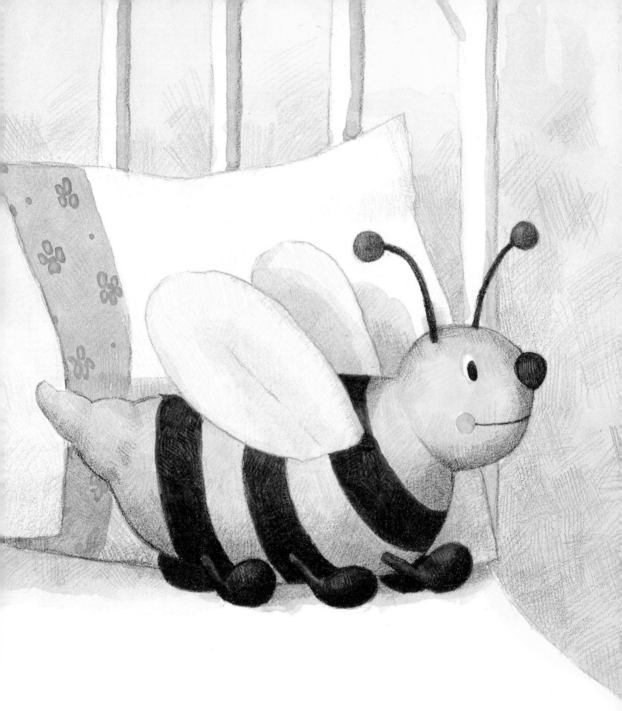

Here is my bee.

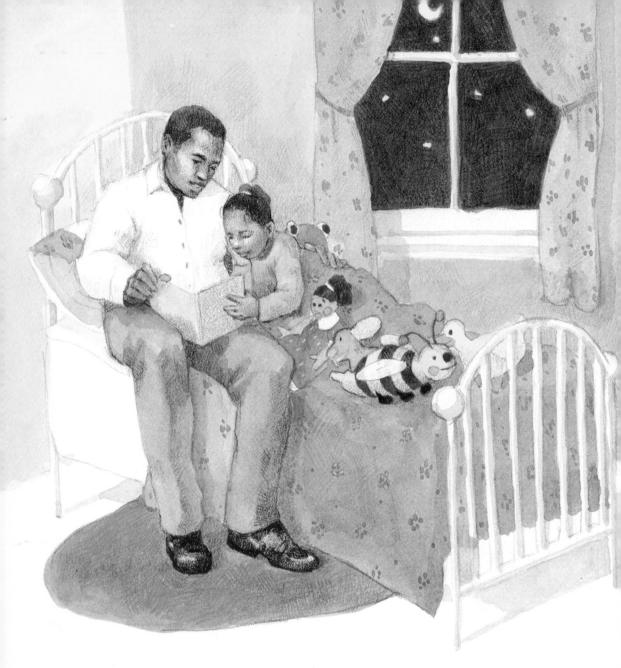

Here is my dad,
and here is me.